Wolves

by Kathleen W. Kranking and Rhonda Lucas Donald

S C H O L A S T I C
PROFESSIONAL BOOKS

NEW YORK • TORONTO • LONDON • AUCKLAND • SYDNEY
MEXICO CITY • NEW DELHI • HONG KONG • BUENOS AIRES

Cover design by Norma Ortiz
Cover photograph © Gerard Lacz/Peter Arnold, Inc.
Interior design by Solutions by Design, Inc.
Interior illustrations by Patricia J. Wynne
Poster design by Norma Ortiz and Adrian Avilés
Photo research by Sarah Longacre
Edited by Ingrid Blinken

ISBN: 0-439-24118-9

Contents

    🐺 = Activities with student reproducibles

How to Use This Book

Welcome to Wolves!

Your students will have a howling good time learning about wolves through the cross-curricular activities in this book! Kids may at first be frightened of "the big, bad wolf." But fright will soon be out of sight once kids learn the true nature of these intelligent social animals. This in-depth resource provides background information, creative activities, hands-on reproducibles, and a giant, colorful poster—everything you need for a wild and wonderful unit on wolves. Before you begin your investigation of wolves, here are a few helpful tips for using this book.

1. Separate facts from fairy tales.

Like many large predators, wolves are often misunderstood. Far from being the man-eaters of fairy tales, wolves are actually shy, intelligent animals that live in close family groups in much the same way people do. The activities in this book will help your students separate the fairy tales from the facts. Before beginning your wolf studies, ask kids to write down three words that describe wolves. They should keep the list until the end of the unit. After they've learned about wolves, kids can review their lists to see which of their descriptions were closer to fact than to fiction.

2. Cross the curriculum with wolves.

Browse through the activities and select those you feel will meet your students' interests, suit their learning styles, and address the content areas you want to teach. Whether you use the activities as they are or adapt and amend them is entirely up to you.

3. Read all about wolves.

Be sure to have lots of fiction and nonfiction books on hand to pique students' interest in reading about wolves. You can set aside a time each day for wolf reading. You might even decide to set up a special corner of your room as a reading "den." Throughout the activities in this book, you'll find Book Breaks—brief reviews of books about wolves, with suggested activities to enhance the reading experience. See the Wolf Resources section at the end of the book for other great reading materials and additional resources.

4. Teach with the "Meet My Family!" poster.

Show students the poster and ask them to point out the wolf. Then introduce them to the other wolf relatives on the poster, including the basset hound. Knowing that dogs and wolves are closely related will fascinate many children. Discuss the similarities and differences among the canines featured on the poster. Read the text aloud. Display the poster near your reading den.

5. Help alleviate wolf woes.

As your class will learn, wolves often fall prey to some sinister stereotypes. Ironically, it is we humans who pose a serious threat to wolves, not the other way around. In fact, they need our help if they're going to survive. Your students can help dispel the myths surrounding wolves by educating people about their intelligence, loyalty, and social nature. Be sure to share the crafts, poems, and other materials your students create as part of the study. Once the word is out that wolves are wonderful, perhaps more people will be willing to help them thrive.

Background Information

Meet the Wolves!

What do your students think of when they hear the word *wolf*? A snarling man-eater? We hope not, but chances are that children are most familiar with this inaccurate portrayal. From movies to fairy tales, the wolf is a victim of its big, bad image.

That image, however, is largely undeserved. In rare instances wolves have attacked people, but for the most part they are shy animals that avoid human contact. It is our hope that as people become more educated about wolves, they will no longer fear them but rather come to appreciate and respect them.

Wolves are found mostly in wilderness areas of northern North America and in parts of Europe, the Middle East, and Asia. There are two species: the gray wolf, which is the largest of all the dogs, and the red wolf. Wolves are members of the *Canidae*, or dog family. Some of their relatives, like the golden retriever and German Shepherd, have been domesticated; others, such as foxes, jackals, and dingoes, remain wild like wolves. As your class moves through this unit, students will notice many similarities between wolves and their own pet dogs.

As a wolf walks through snow, its toes spread out so that its feet function like snowshoes.

It is a myth that wolves howl at the moon.

The Hair of the Wolf

From its pointed snout to the tip of its tail, a wolf is covered with beautiful hair. Despite their name, gray wolves are not necessarily gray. They range in color from white to gray to black. Red wolves are cinnamon to deep rust with gray or black highlights. Whatever their color, wolf hairs come in two types. The long, coarse outer hairs, called guard hairs, shed water from the wolf's coat. The soft, downy undercoat provides a warm layer of insulation during cold months. During the spring and summer, wolves shed their hair in clumps.

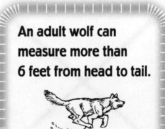

An adult wolf can measure more than 6 feet from head to tail.

The Better to Smell You

A wolf's keen senses of sight and hearing help it to be an efficient predator. But, as with other members of the dog family, the wolf is most dependent upon its sense of smell, both in hunting prey and in social relationships. Above the roof of a wolf's mouth is a pouchlike organ lined with about 200 million "smelling cells."

All this smelling power enables a wolf to smell its prey more than a mile away.

A wolf's sense of smell is about 100 times more acute than a human's.

What Big Teeth You Have

When children are asked to draw a picture of a wolf, most will exaggerate the wolf's fangs. These impressive teeth may have helped to inspire the wolf's fearsome image. The fangs are the largest of the wolf's 42 teeth (that's 10 teeth more than a person has), measuring $2\frac{1}{4}$ inches from root to tip. When the wolf clamps down its strong jaws, the top and bottom fangs interlock to allow the wolf to hang on to struggling prey. Farther back in the wolf's mouth are immense molars, which are designed for crushing bones and grinding meat.

Wolves use all these teeth to hunt and eat a variety of foods. Their usual prey consists of moose, deer, and caribou. Because of the large size of these animals, wolves hunt them in packs. The larger the pack, the bigger the prey it will capture. Wolves usually target animals that are young,

The stomach of an adult wolf can hold up to 20 pounds of meat—the equivalent of about 80 hamburgers!

old, or sick. Lone wolves, those that are not part of a pack, must eat what they can catch themselves. Often they survive on smaller animals such as rodents, birds, or beavers. Sometimes wolves will even eat carrion (the flesh of an animal that has already been killed) or vegetation.

A wolf may eat only once in four days, and it can go as long as two weeks without eating.

Life in a Pack

A wolf can weigh anywhere from 40 to 175 pounds.

Your students may know that wolves live in packs, but they may not realize how similar a wolf pack is to a human family. A pack is made up of a mother, father, siblings of the parents, pups of different ages, and sometimes even a grandparent. The parent wolves, called the alpha male and female, lead the pack and are usually the only wolves in the pack that breed. They often mate for life. Sometimes, however, a pack may have only one alpha animal—like a single-parent family. A pack usually has about eight members, but pack size can vary depending on the availability and size of prey. In areas where a pack's main prey is moose, for example, there may be as many as 20 members. Each member

must obey the alphas and afford them certain rights such as eating first after a kill.

A wolf pack is organized in a social hierarchy beneath the alpha pair. Grown pups of one or two years are higher than young pups. Young pups in turn are higher than the designated "babysitter" wolves, which care for the pups while the rest of the pack is off hunting. The lowest-ranking members of the pack are called the omega wolves.

Young wolves establish their rank within the pack through play fighting and grow up to become either "biders" or "dispersers." Biders are submissive wolves that bide their time waiting to move up in the pack or even to take over the pack's territory if the alpha pair dies. Dispersers are more dominant wolves that leave the pack and strike out on their own. These lone wolves search for a mate and their own territory. The pack's hierarchy ensures its survival. If the wolves do not work cooperatively, they cannot raise their young or hunt successfully.

Home Sweet Home

Each wolf pack has a home range called a territory. Territories vary in size—generally, the larger the wolf pack, the larger the territory. Territories are usually big enough to provide about 10 square miles per wolf. Wolf territories often overlap, but packs usually avoid contact with one another. Lone wolves don't have territories; instead they skirt the buffer zones around other wolves' territories.

Wolf packs use scent markers along the borders of their territory to tell other wolf packs to stay away. Scent marks can be made with urine or feces, or by rubbing the body against an object such as a tree or scratching in the dirt. These scented messages are usually left in prominent places—tree stumps, rocks, or snowbanks. They serve as "No Trespassing" signs to other wolves.

Members of a pack also use scent marks to communicate within the pack. For example, markers serve as boundary reminders to young wolves that are learning to identify their territory. They can also be left as messages to pack members that have been separated from the others.

Communication, Wolf-Style

The hierarchy within a wolf pack is maintained through "wolf language," which includes scent marking, vocalizations, body postures, and facial expressions. Some of this communication is universal and would be understood by any wolf, and some is understandable only within a particular pack.

Wolves are famous for their "singing," but howls are only one of several types of wolf vocalizations. They also bark, whimper, and growl, and each of these types of communication can in turn

A wolf can hear other wolves howling several miles away.

consist of various sounds—for example, whimpers can include whines, squeaks, or squeals. Generally speaking, whimpers indicate friendliness and submission, whereas squeals connote caring.

Wolves can run 25 to 40 miles an hour when chasing prey.

Wolves howl for many different reasons. A wolf may howl when it is separated from the pack or when trying to warn wolves from other packs to stay away. Sometimes wolves howl when they want to assemble the pack; other times they seem to howl just for fun. They have also been known to howl in response to train whistles and sirens.

Wolves can hear howls over great distances. They can tell the exact location of a howling wolf and can readily identify not only the significance of the howl but also the identity of the howler, much in the same way we can recognize people by their voices. What's more, wolves can distinguish recorded howls from live ones.

In addition to vocalization, wolves communicate using facial expressions and body postures that convey a variety of messages. Being able to communicate in these ways reduces the chances of physical conflict within the pack. Most of the communication among wolves signals either dominance or submission, depending on the social position of the wolves involved. Dominant postures usually make the wolf appear bigger and more aggressive. The hairs on its back, ears, and neck stand up; it stiffens its legs to look taller; and it stares aggressively with its teeth bared. Dominant wolves will hold their tails high and point their ears forward. Submissive postures have the opposite effect. A submissive wolf may cower, lie down, or roll over. It flattens its ears against its head, tucks its tail between its legs, and pulls its lips back into a smile. Of course, some communication is neither dominant nor submissive—for example, during play or friendly greetings.

Problems for Wolves

Next to humans, the gray wolf was once the most widespread mammal outside the tropics. As recently as 150 years ago, gray wolves were plentiful across North America. But hatred of the wolf led to its decline. People feared wolves because of the untrue stories that were told about them, and they feared for their livestock, upon which wolves sometimes preyed. In an effort to eradicate the wolf, the animals were poisoned, shot, and trapped until their numbers began to dwindle. Habitat destruction caused by human development of the land also led to the decline of the wolf. Today the gray and red wolves are endangered species.

But there's good news about wolves too—they're making a comeback! Thanks to reintroduction efforts, gray wolves have returned to Yellowstone National Park after more than 60 years. And red wolves now roam free again in the southeastern United States for the first time in 100 years. Reintroducing wolves requires substantial effort and resources as well as cooperation from people in areas near reintroduction sites. Luckily, the more people learn about wolves, the more inclined they are to contribute to the preservation of these fascinating creatures.

Student Activities

All in the Family
(CRITICAL THINKING, SCIENCE)

*Students compare and contrast wolves
with other canids.*

Use the poster to help children compare
wolves with their canid relatives. Look at each
of the animals shown. Ask children to point
out similarities among the animals (teeth,
paws, tails, pointed noses, and so on). Then
look at the differences (fur length, color, and
pattern; size of body; size of ears; length of
legs). Next, show kids pictures of other
animals such as raccoons, bears, and deer.
How do these animals compare to wolves?

Distribute a copy of page 19 to each
student. Explain that students will make a
guest list for a canine family reunion. Read
through the names on the sheet. Have children
circle the canines to show who can come.
Remind them to look for the characteristics
you discussed.

ANSWERS: basset hound, dingo, red fox,
coyote, Simien jackal, and raccoon dog are all
canids. The skunk , brown bear, and raccoon
are not.

 Brother Wolf: A Seneca Tale, by
Harriet P. Taylor (Farrar Straus &
Giroux, 1996), is a *pourquoi* tale.
(A pourquoi tale explains why something is the
way it is—for example, why a leopard has
spots.) This tale explains why some birds have
beautifully colored feathers and how a
raccoon's penchant for pranks led to his having
a striped tail. Share other pourquoi tales with
your class (such as Rudyard Kipling's *Just So
Stories*), and encourage children to write or
dictate pourquoi stories of their own.

More Poster Fun
(LANGUAGE ARTS, SCIENCE)

*Students learn about wolves and their
relatives.*

Ask students the following questions as they
look at the poster:

- Which dog's name rhymes with *Ringo*?
  (dingo)
- Which wolf isn't really a wolf at all? (the
  maned wolf)
- Which is the smallest dog? (fennec fox)
- Which dog is a famous cartoon character?
  (Warner Brothers' Wile E. Coyote)
- Which dog is a common pet? (basset
  hound)
- Which dog has long legs? (the maned wolf)
- How many dogs can you count on the
  poster? How many legs do you think there
  are? How do you know? (6 dogs; 24 legs)

Wolf Tales
(ART, LANGUAGE ARTS)

*Students separate wolf facts from fiction
as they read wolf stories and write wolf
stories.*

Stories about wolves tell us a lot about how
people view these animals. Many stories, such
as *Little Red Riding Hood* and *The Three
Little Pigs*, paint wolves in a negative light by
portraying them as bloodthirsty, cunning
killers. Happily, not all wolf stories are so
unflattering. American Indian tales, such as

those in *Wolf Tales: Native American Children's Stories*, edited by Mary Powell (Ancient City Press, 1993), and *Brother Wolf: A Seneca Tale*, by Harriet P. Taylor (see Book Break on page 9), pay tribute to wolves' intelligence, strength, and loyalty. As you share wolf stories from both European and Native American traditions, ask students to consider how wolves are portrayed in each piece. Why do they think Europeans feared wolves and Native Americans revered them? (Consider the lifestyles of the two cultures for clues.)

Next, share a fun wolf story that turns a fairy tale on its ear: Jon Scieszka's *The True Story of the 3 Little Pigs* (Puffin, 1996). Once children have had a chance to become better acquainted with wolves through these readings and your study as a whole, ask them to create a class book that describes wolves in words and pictures.

Give each student a copy of page 20. Read the rhyme aloud to the class, and give kids time to write or dictate a short story that highlights their favorite wolf fact(s). Collect the pages and bind them with yarn or string to create a collaborative class book.

Musical Interlude

Sergei Prokofiev's *Peter and the Wolf* provides an opportunity to examine how wolves are portrayed in a piece of music. After reviewing the story with students (see page 32 for a suggested book), listen to the piece and discuss the instruments used to represent Peter, the wolf, and other characters in the story. How do the instruments' sounds help define the characters they represent? What is the mood of the music when the wolf is featured? Listening to *Peter and the Wolf* affords a great chance to familiarize students with instruments and the tones and moods they can evoke.

Where in the World Are the Wolves?
(GEOGRAPHY, MATH)

Students look at a world map and answer questions to help them see where wolves are living today.

Where are all the wolves? All you'll need to help your students answer that question is a large map of the world and 18 copies of the wolf on page 11.

What to Do:

1 Review the Countries Where Wolves Live list below with your students. As you locate each country on the map, label it with a paper wolf.

2 Then, rather than tell students how many wolves live in each place, have them use the Country Clues on page 11 to discover which country is home to the most wolves today.

COUNTRIES WHERE WOLVES LIVE

(Numbers in parentheses are estimated wolf population figures from 1999 and come from the International Wolf Center in Ely, Minnesota. In some cases, population ranges have been averaged or rounded.)

Bangladesh (550)	India (1,400)
Bosnia (800)	Israel (150)
Bulgaria (900)	Italy (425)
Canada (60,000)	Mongolia (30,000)
China (6,000)	Romania (2,500)
Croatia (75)	Russia (30,000)
Ethiopia (550)	Saudi Arabia (650)
Germany (7)	Spain (2,000)
Greenland (60)	United States (11,500)

COUNTRY CLUES

1. It's not a country that begins with an *E* or an *S*.

2. It's not a European country.

3. It's not an island.

4. It's not an Asian or Middle Eastern country.

5. It's not the United States.

ANSWER: Canada has the most wolves—about 60,000.

Note: Younger students may have difficulty grasping the large numbers in this activity. You may want to focus only on where wolves live and which country has the most wolves. If you choose to introduce the wolf populations of each country, you might color-code the wolves you place on the map so that each one stands for a different number. For example, each gray wolf might represent 10,000 wolves; each black wolf, 1,000 wolves; and each brown wolf, 100 wolves. You can even cut wolf shapes in half, quarters, and so on, to represent fractions of the amount. You might also want to show wolf populations on a graph instead of on the map.

Terrific Teeth
(SCIENCE)

Students observe how a wolf's teeth help it hold on to prey.

Look at a picture of a wolf with its mouth open and you'll notice the long, sharp canine teeth right away. These fearsome-looking teeth enable the wolf to puncture the skin of its prey. The wolf then sinks its teeth into the flesh so that its meal cannot get away.

The following activity helps demonstrate the effectiveness of such teeth. Since the activity requires a staple remover, perform the demonstration yourself as students observe.

What You'll Need:

🐾 piece of cloth

🐾 staple remover

🐾 oven mitt

What to Do:

1 Hold on to the piece of cloth and explain that it represents the wolf's prey.

2 Explain that the staple remover represents a wolf with its sharp canine teeth. Have the "wolf" take a bite of its "prey" by grasping the cloth with the staple remover.

3 Let kids try to pull the cloth free to show how well the teeth hang on. To emphasize this point, instead use an oven mitt to represent the wolf's teeth. This time students should be able to free the piece of cloth with ease.

 BOOK BREAK *The Fascinating World of Wolves*, by Maria Ángels Julivert (Barrons, 1996), is an excellent overview of wolf anatomy, social structure, and natural history. The book's illustrations are excellent springboards for discussion, especially when viewed along with photographs from other works such as *Scruffy: A Wolf Finds His Place in the Pack* (Walker & Co., 1996) and *To the Top of the World: Adventures With Arctic Wolves* (Walker & Co. 1995), both by Jim Brandenburg. Ask students to consider how effectively each medium depicts wolves and their surroundings.

Hair of the Dog
(ART, SCIENCE)

Students make earmuffs to help them understand how a wolf's fur helps it survive.

Purchase some furry swatches or felt from your local fabric or craft store. Be sure to get fur in a variety of wolf colors (see page 5 for more information about wolf fur). As children examine the fur, ask them to consider the ways in which it helps wolves survive (camouflage, protection from wetness and cold). Ask how, for example, having white fur would be beneficial to a wolf living in a snowy region. It will also be important for children to realize that a wolf's fur is its sole means of protection from the elements. Explain that unlike humans, wolves do not put on different kinds of clothes for different types of weather. Their fur helps keep them warm and dry. In warmer months they may shed some fur to prevent them from being too warm, but in winter their fur is all they have to keep them from being cold.

To help students appreciate how warm wolf fur can be, invite each student to make a pair of furry earmuffs, following the directions below.

What You'll Need:

- copies of the earmuff template (page 13)
- thin cardboard
- pens
- scissors
- furry fabric or felt
- glue
- 36-inch lengths of ribbon ($\frac{1}{2}$ to 1 inch wide, one per student)
- two pairs of wiggle eyes per student

What to Do:

1 Cut out the earmuff template and then trace around it twice on thin cardboard. Cut out the shapes.

2 Trace and cut out the shapes again, this time on the furry fabric or felt. Each student will need four furry wolf heads.

3 Lay the cardboard shapes on a flat surface with the ears facing each other, as shown. Then lay the ribbon across the shapes, being sure to allow enough slack so that the wolf shapes easily reach both ears. Glue the ribbon into place. (There should be about 8 or 9 inches of ribbon between the two ear pieces, depending on each child's head size. Children will need help with this step.)

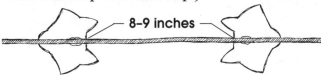

4 Cover the cardboad shapes with a thin layer of glue. Attach a layer of fur or felt to each ear piece.

5 After a few minutes, flip the shapes over, cover the other side with a thin layer of glue, and glue the remaining fabric shapes in place.

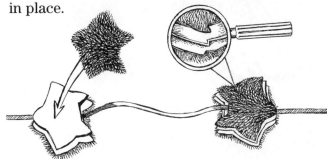

6 Glue on the eyes. Let the glue dry completely before trying on the earmuffs.

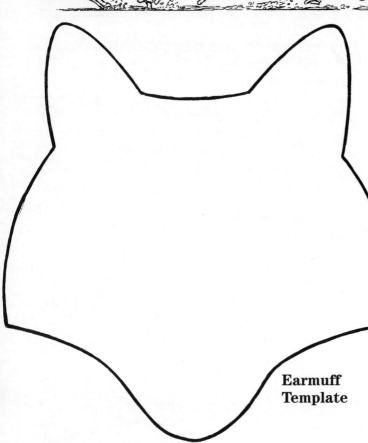

**Earmuff
Template**

Super Sniffers
(SCIENCE)

*Conduct a simple experiment to help
students appreciate the strength of a wolf's
sense of smell.*

What You'll Need:

🐾 two small paper or plastic cups

🐾 an eyedropper

🐾 water

🐾 isopropyl (rubbing) alcohol

What to Do:

1 Have students count along as you put 100
drops of water into one cup.

2 Squeeze one drop of alcohol into the other
cup.

3 Have each child smell both liquids. The
water will be odorless; children should be
able to smell the alcohol easily.

4 Put one drop of alcohol into the cup
of water and stir. Ask students to
predict how easy it will be to smell the
alcohol now. Have children smell the
mixture.

5 Explain to the class that though we
can no longer smell the alcohol once
it has been diluted in water, a wolf would
be able to because its sense of smell is
100 times stronger than our own.

Paws for Thought
(CRITICAL THINKING, MEASUREMENT, SCIENCE)

*Students compare a wolf paw with a
human hand and try to walk like a wolf.*

Give each child a copy of page 21 and a
ruler. The illustration shows an average
sized front-foot paw print that measures
approximately $4\frac{1}{2}$ inches by $3\frac{3}{4}$ inches. As
students follow the directions on the
reproducible, invite them to compare and
contrast their hand with a wolf's paw. Ask them
to consider what functions the various parts of
the hand and paw serve. Our fingers, for
example, are made for grasping and holding, so
they are fairly long. Wolves' paws, however, are
made for running, so their toes are short.
Encourage students to record their observations
in the spaces provided on the activity sheet.

To deepen children's understanding of how
wolves' padded paws help them survive, give
each child a sponge that is large enough to
cover one of their hands. Secure the sponge
with string. Let the children "walk" their hands
across a tabletop. Ask: "Which hand makes
more noise? Which hand feels more
cushioned?" Children should find that the hand
with the sponge offers more cushioning and
muffles sound much better than the hand
without the sponge. Ask children to consider
why these types of protection are so important
to wolves.

Talk Like a Wolf
(ART, SCIENCE)

Students make wolf masks with movable ears and snouts to illustrate facial expressions and their meanings.

Explain that, like people, wolves have very expressive faces. By looking at the position of a wolf's ears and mouth, you can tell what its expression communicates. Share the following wolf expressions with your students, and then help them make masks to illustrate these and other expressions.

Neutral

Happy

Apologetic

Angry

What You'll Need:

- thin paper plates (2 to 3 per student)
- scissors
- hole punch
- brass fasteners
- string (two 12-inch pieces per student)
- markers
- tape or staples
- red construction paper

What to Do:

1 To make the chin, trim a round paper plate as shown. Cut out holes for the eyes about $1\frac{1}{2}$ inches apart in the center of the plate.

2 Cut out two ears from a second paper plate. Use a hole punch and brass fasteners to attach the ears to the mask, as shown.

3 Punch two more holes on each side of the mask and tie a piece of string through each one.

4 Draw teeth and color the mask (optional).

5 Cut out the upper snout from another piece of paper plate and draw a nose on top.

6 Make the wolf's tongue out of red construction paper.

7 Before you attach the snout and tongue as shown, be sure to insert the tongue between the snout parts and check that all parts are aligned properly.

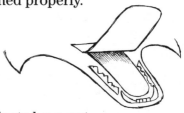

8 Once students have put on their masks, have them experiment with ear and snout positions to communicate different wolf messages.

Time to Howl!
(MUSIC, SCIENCE)

Students sing a song to learn about different wolf vocalizations and their meanings.

After reviewing Communication, Wolf-Style (pages 7–8), give each student a copy of "Time to Howl!" (page 22). Sing the song for children a few times to the tune of "If You're Happy and You Know It." Encourage them to join in when they feel comfortable. Once everyone has learned the lyrics, invite students to add some movements to the song as well.

Follow the Pack Leader
(MOVEMENT, SCIENCE)

Students don their wolf masks and play a version of Follow the Leader to experience life in the pack.

Playing a game of Follow the Leader is a great way to emphasize the role of the alpha male as leader of the pack. Encourage students to wear their wolf masks from the activity on page 14. Then choose a pack leader and begin a game of Follow the Leader with a decidedly wolfish slant. Have the alpha do things like run, play, stalk, howl, nap, or anything else real wolves might do. Switch leaders so that other kids have a chance to be the alpha for a while and have the rest of the pack follow their lead.

Then make the game more challenging by sending the pack on a hunt. Hide a stuffed animal or other object in a large open space, such as a field or a gymnasium, allowing a few "wolves" to watch as you do it. Before the other wolves begin hunting, tell them that rather than talk, they must communicate using "wolf speak." (In advance, review with students the information on pages 7–8) The wolves that watched you hide the prey must indicate its location to the others from the sidelines by howling, whining, barking, and so on.

Canine Cafe
(SCIENCE)

Students learn about a wolf's eating habits as they imagine they are wolves ordering a meal at the Canine Cafe.

Remind students that, as predators, wolves kill and eat other animals—big and small—to survive.

Hand out copies of page 23 to each student and review the directions. Note: Buried bison refers to wolves' habit of burying large kills to save for later. Also note that wolves do occasionally eat vegetation—just as dogs will sometimes eat grass—but it is not a significant portion of their diet. For the purposes of this activity, only the "meaty" choices are correct.

ANSWERS: whipped white-tailed deer, roast rabbit, fish fry, bighorn sheep sandwich, duck dumplings, minced mouse, buried bison, moose melt

Wolf Tracks
(MATH, SCIENCE)

Students play a game that simulates using radio signals to track wolves.

A scientist holds an antenna over her head and slowly turns in a circle. At first nothing happens. Then a strong "beep" sounds from the box in her hand. She's located a wolf wearing a radio collar. She quickly writes the direction the signal came from on a map, packs up her gear, drives a mile or so away, and does the same thing. Again, another "beep." She marks the second direction on the map. With the two readings, she can tell where the wolf is. If she tags along after the wolf, she just might find the site of a kill or a den of pups.

Radio tracking is a very important way for scientists to learn about wolves and other

animals. But it is difficult and doesn't always work—for example, trees or hills can distort signals. And if a wolf is too far away, the antenna can't pick up the signal at all. Sometimes scientists have to guess where to start looking for a signal. Using radio signals to search for wolves is a bit like playing a game. Here is your students' chance to get in on the fun.

Wolf Tracks is a variation of the game Bingo. One player is the caller and needs a grid and a pencil. The other players each need a grid (page 24) and four wolf markers (below). Players place the wolves on four different coordinates on their grid. The caller represents the scientist trying to track wolves. The caller chooses a point on the grid and calls out the coordinates (for example, "B, 4"). Players with wolves on that spot say "Beep" and remove the wolves from the board—these wolves have been tracked. The first player to have all of his or her wolves tracked becomes the next caller.

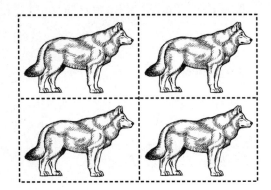

Tips:

- Laminate the game boards and markers for greater durability.

- Have the caller mark each point on the grid as he or she calls out those coordinates.

- You might keep track of how many wolves each caller locates. After several rounds, determine which caller has tracked the most wolves.

Trouble on the Range
(GEOGRAPHY, MATH, SCIENCE)

Students practice their map-reading skills as they develop an understanding of how wolf ranges have shrunk over the years.

As students compare past and present wolf ranges, they can also develop a sense of some fraction basics. You may want to begin by cutting a circle into four equal sections and introducing the concepts of whole, half, quarter, and three-quarters. Explain that a wolf range is an area in which wolves live. Then look at the maps on page 25; one map shows wolf ranges of the past and the other shows present wolf ranges. Antarctica is not shown on either map; wolves have never lived there.

After students have answered the questions on page 26, ask them to consider why the range has shrunken so dramatically. While the reasons are varied, it is important for students to realize how large an impact humans have had on wolves. See page 8 for more information.

ANSWERS:

1. about half
2. about half (Nearly all of the range in the lower 48 states is gone.)
3. less than a quarter
4. between one-half and three-quarters
5. Africa, Antarctica (not shown on map), Australia, South America
6. Asia, Europe, North America

The Game of Wolf Life
(MATH, SCIENCE)

Students play a board game to learn more about wolf survival.

The Game of Wolf Life is based on the true life story of wolves that were reintroduced into Yellowstone Park. As your students play, they

will come to understand the kinds of obstacles and opportunities these wolves faced. The game is designed for 2–4 players.

What You'll Need:

🐾 1 game board (pages 28–29)

🐾 4 playing pieces (page 27)

🐾 number cube (page 27)

🐾 markers or crayons

🐾 file folder (optional)

Assembling the Game:

1 Make a copy of the game board, number cube, and four playing pieces. Have students color the game board and playing pieces. Cut the game board along the dotted line and tape the two halves together. (You may want to laminate the game board and glue it inside a file folder.)

2 Cut out the number cube and fold along the dotted lines. Glue or tape together to assemble the cube.

3 Cut out the playing pieces along the solid lines (including the short solid line between the two FOLD tabs). Fold along the dotted lines so that the wolves face out and the tabs at the bottom allow the piece to stand. Glue or tape the two sides together.

How to Play:

1 Players place their playing pieces in the den and then roll the number cube to determine who goes first.

2 The first player rolls the number cube and moves forward that number of spaces. The player reads aloud the directions in the space and follows them. If directed to do so, the player moves his or her playing piece ahead or back the appropriate number of spaces. The player does not follow the directions in the new space. The next player takes a turn.

3 Players continue to take turns until one wolf reaches the end to become the pack leader.

Internet Interlude

To help your students see how real wolf trackers do their job, visit "Wild Animal Watch: Wolves" at **http://teacher. scholastic.com/wolves**. Here kids can read interviews with wolf scientists, learn wolf facts, listen to wolf howls, view artwork featuring wolves, and read scientists' journals about their work and experiences with both red and gray wolves.

Return of the Wolf
(CURRENT EVENTS, GEOGRAPHY, LANGUAGE ARTS, SCIENCE)

Students do research and write articles about wolf reintroduction.

Throughout North America, wolf populations are making a comeback. Over the years, packs have survived in Isle Royale in Lake Superior, in Mexico's Sierra Madre, and in the southeastern United States. Some Canadian wolves have even migrated back into Montana. In 1995 the U.S. Fish and Wildlife Service reintroduced Canadian wolves into Yellowstone National Park in Idaho. Similar though less successful reintroductions have taken place in Arizona and New Mexico.

Help students locate on a map the areas that are currently populated by wolves. Then invite them to research the triumphs and trials of the reintroduction efforts, for both wolves and their human neighbors. Support students' efforts by asking questions, such as: "Where has reintroduction been the most successful? What kinds of challenges has the process presented? What might happen to wolves if their population levels were to bounce back enough to remove them from the endangered species list?"

After doing the research, kids can write articles detailing their findings.

Save the Wolves Campaign
(ART, MATH, LANGUAGE ARTS)

Now that your students have learned many fascinating things about wolves, it's their turn to teach others to respect and protect them.

People's negative attitudes toward wolves may be one of the biggest reasons their populations have declined in many places. Before people can devote themselves to protecting wolves and their habitat, they must learn that wolves aren't the evil killers the fairy tales make them out to be. What better way for students to share their newfound knowledge than through a class campaign to save the wolves? Here are some ideas to get you started, whether you launch your campaign during Wolf Awareness Week (the third week of October) or at another time of the year.

Wolf Survey—Come up with several simple questions for students to ask friends and family to determine their opinions and knowledge about wolves. You can use the survey results to decide which of the following activities might best help people in your community better understand wolves.

Community Displays—Check with your local library or other community facility about setting up a wolf display that features students' efforts to encourage others to help save the wolves.

Wolf Bites—Publish a short wolf newspaper to distribute to your school community. The paper could include brief articles about wolves and the dangers they face as well as students' drawings, cartoons, and poems.

Wolf Web—Create your own Web page featuring what your class has learned about wolves. Free step-by-step Web design help can be found at the Filamentality Web site at **www.kn.pacbell.com/wired/fil/index.html**

Wolf Party—Invite family and friends to see all your class has learned about wolves. Once children have had a chance to share their work, show a wolf video such as National Geographic's *Wolves: A Legend Returns to Yellowstone* or Discovery's *Wolves at Our Door*. If you can, invite a wolf specialist to come and speak to your students and classroom visitors. You might even want to serve some wolf-inspired refreshments, such as wolf-shaped cookies, cupcakes with wolves on top, or spreads on wolf-shaped bread.

Adopt a Wolf—You and your class may choose to adopt a wolf through one of the organizations mentioned on page 32. Once you've adopted a wolf, you'll receive photos of the animal as well as periodic updates. Proceeds from the adoption go toward wolf conservation.

The Evening Howl
(LANGUAGE ARTS, SCIENCE)

Students sniff out more wolf news and solve puzzles in the latest edition of The Evening Howl.

News Worth Howling About

Distribute copies of pages 30–31 to students. First, read aloud the news stories on the front page. Then lead a discussion about the issues involved.

Wolf Puzzles

ANSWERS:

Blaze a Trail Home

Word Scramble
1—H, 2—O ,
3—W, 4—L

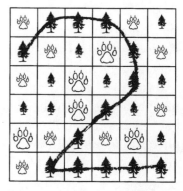

Name _____ Date _____

All in the Family

The wolves are planning a canine family reunion, but they need your help figuring out whom to invite. Circle the canines below to show who is invited. (Hint: Three of the animals are not canines.)

basset hound

dingo

red fox

coyote

skunk

Simien jackal

brown bear

raccoon dog

raccoon

Name _____ Date _____

Wolf Tales

Read the poem below. Then choose your favorite wolf fact and write your own short story about it.

Some tales say wolves are big and scary.
They flash sharp teeth and are very hairy!
Some tales say wolves are brave and wise.
They look on wolves with kinder eyes.
Some wolf tales will make you smile,
Or teach a lesson all the while.
I'd like to tell a wolf tale, too—
One that's just the facts—it's true!

Here is my wolf story: _____

_____

_____

_____

_____

_____

Wolves Scholastic Professional Books

Paws for Thought

Use a ruler to measure the wolf paw.

How long is the paw? _____

How wide is it? _____

Trace your own hand on the back of this sheet.

How long is your hand? _____

How wide is it? _____

How is a wolf's paw similar to your hand?

_____

How is it different?

_____

_____

Our fingers help us hold things. What do you think the different parts of a wolf's paw help it do?

_____

_____

Name _____ Date _____

Time to Howl!

(Sung to the tune of "If You're Happy and You Know It")

When the pack has made a kill, it's time to howl.
Owooooo! (Make howling sound.)
When the pack has made a kill, it's time to howl.
Owooooo!
When the pack has made a kill, all the members get their fill.
When the pack has made a kill, it's time to howl.
Owooooo!

When there's danger somewhere close, a wolf will bark.
Bark! Bark!
When there's danger somewhere close, a wolf will bark.
Bark! Bark!
When there's danger somewhere close, all the others need to know.
When there's danger somewhere close, a wolf will bark.
Bark! Bark!

When a wolf would like to play, it's whimper time.
Mmmm-mmm! (Make whimpering sound.)
When a wolf would like to play, it's whimper time.
Mmmm-mmm!
When a wolf would like to play, a whimper helps it gets its way.
When a wolf would like to play, it's whimper time.
Mmmm-mmm!

When a wolf gets really mad, it gives a growl.
Grrrrr-rrrrrr!
When a wolf gets really mad, it gives a growl.
Grrrrr-rrrrrr!
When a wolf gets really mad—or another wolf is bad—
When a wolf gets really mad, it gives a growl.
Grrrrr-rrrrrr!

Wolves Scholastic Professional Books

Canine Cafe

Welcome to the Canine Cafe! Imagine that you're a wolf ordering a meal. Circle all the foods on the menu that would make a tasty meal for a wolf.

whipped white-tailed deer

carrot cake

moose melt

roast rabbit

buried bison

fish fry

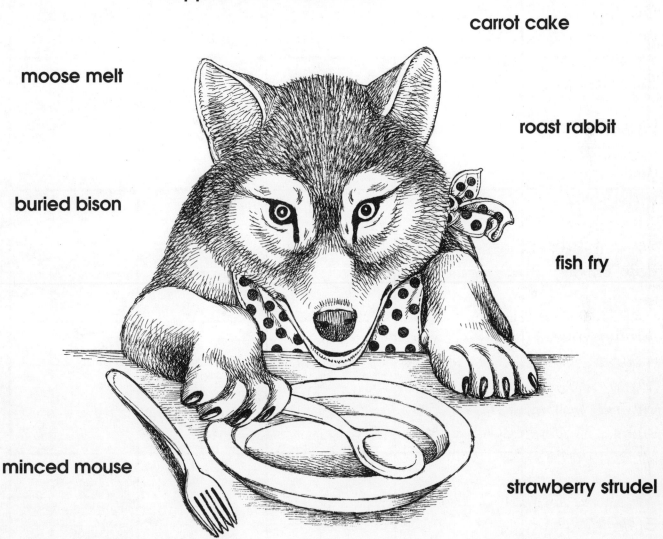

minced mouse

strawberry strudel

browned tree bark

bighorn sheep sandwich

duck dumplings

Wolf Tracks

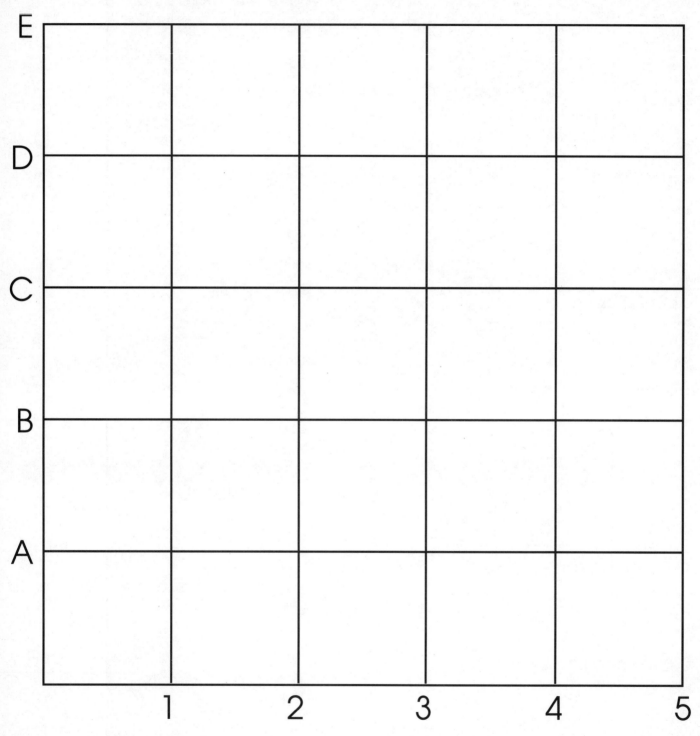

Name _____ Date _____

Trouble on the Range

This map shows where wolves used to live.

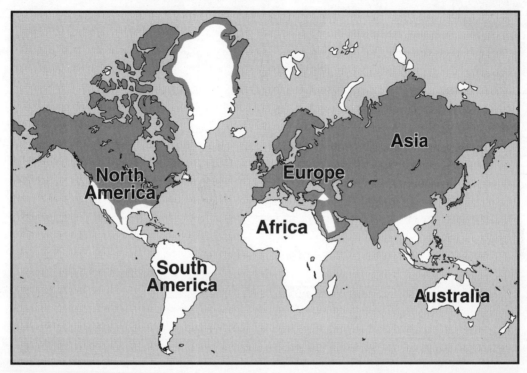

This map shows where wolves live today. Use the two maps to answer the questions on the next page.

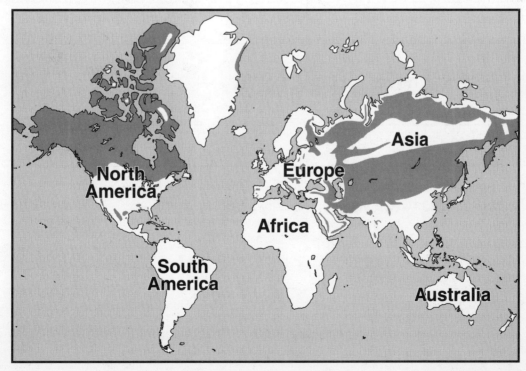

Name _____ Date _____

Trouble on the Range

1. About how much of the original wolf range is left today?

_____

_____

2. About how much range is left in North America?

_____

_____

3. About how much range still exists in Europe?

_____

_____

4. About how much range is still in Asia?

_____

_____

5. Which continents never had any wolves?

_____

_____

6. Which continents have wolves today?

_____

_____

Wolves Scholastic Professional Books

The Game of Wolf Life
Playing Pieces and Number Cube

FOLD   FOLD

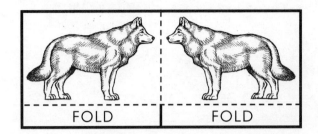

FOLD   FOLD

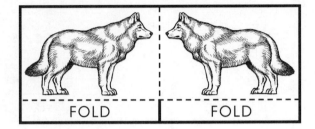

FOLD   FOLD

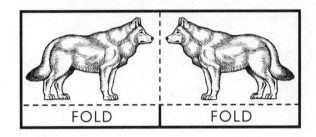

FOLD   FOLD

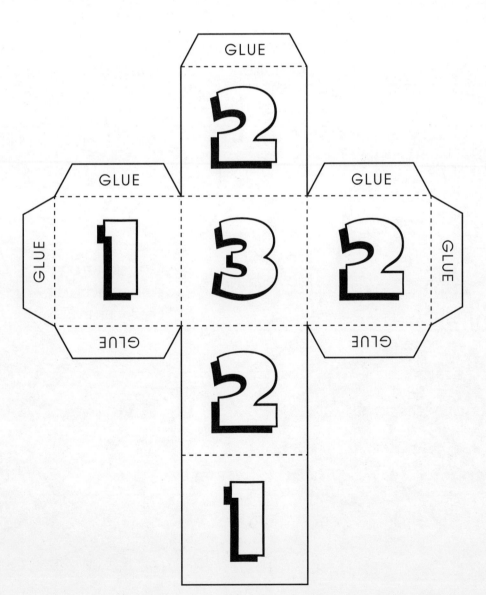

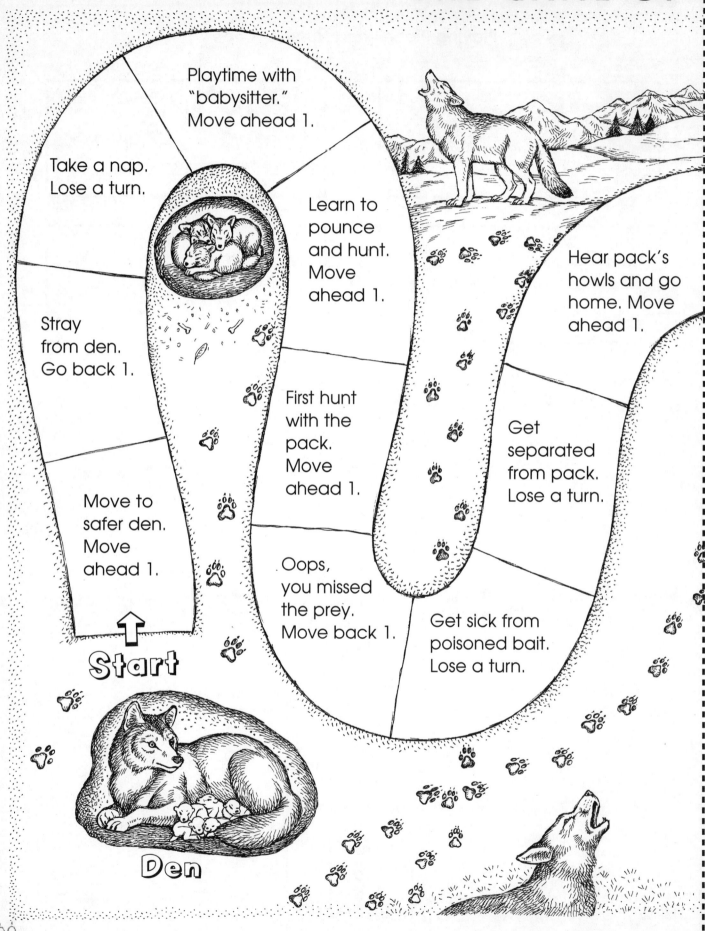

Playtime with "babysitter." Move ahead 1.

Take a nap. Lose a turn.

Learn to pounce and hunt. Move ahead 1.

Hear pack's howls and go home. Move ahead 1.

Stray from den. Go back 1.

First hunt with the pack. Move ahead 1.

Get separated from pack. Lose a turn.

Move to safer den. Move ahead 1.

Oops, you missed the prey. Move back 1.

Get sick from poisoned bait. Lose a turn.

Start

Den

WOLF LIFE

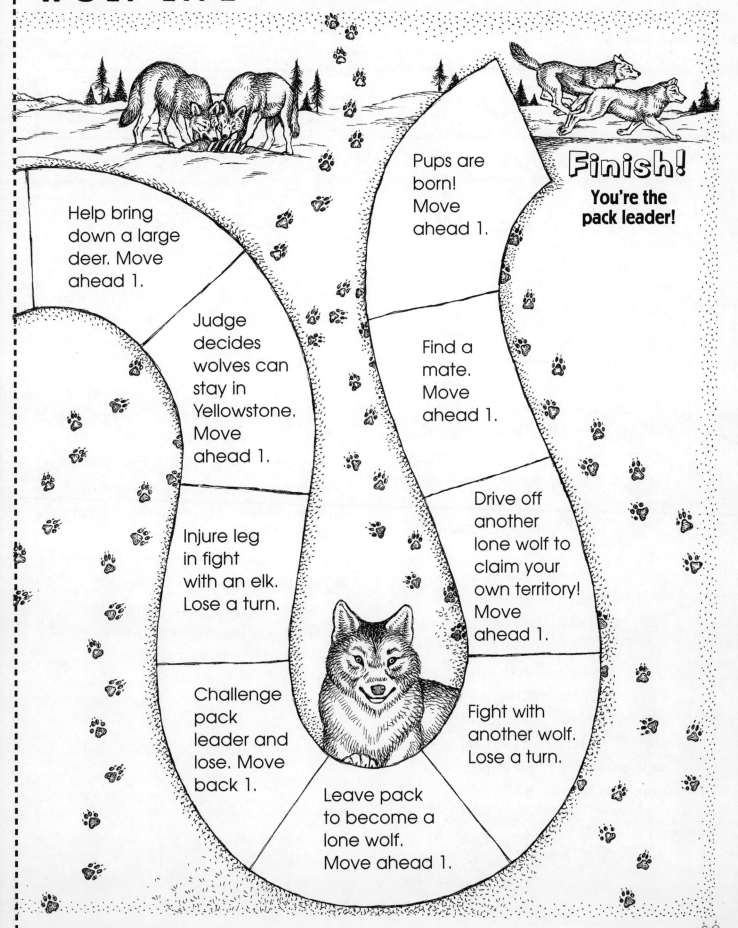

Help bring down a large deer. Move ahead 1.

Judge decides wolves can stay in Yellowstone. Move ahead 1.

Injure leg in fight with an elk. Lose a turn.

Challenge pack leader and lose. Move back 1.

Leave pack to become a lone wolf. Move ahead 1.

Pups are born! Move ahead 1.

Find a mate. Move ahead 1.

Drive off another lone wolf to claim your own territory! Move ahead 1.

Fight with another wolf. Lose a turn.

Finish!
You're the pack leader!

Name _____ Date _____

The Evening Howl

NEWS WORTH HOWLING ABOUT

Wolves Are Back!

Two hundred years ago, gray and red wolves lived in many parts of the United States. But people back then didn't like wolves at all. They were afraid of wolves. They killed as many wolves as they could. People also took over the land where the wolves lived. This also made it hard for wolves to survive. Now both gray and red wolves are endangered.

Luckily, the story does not end there. Now people are helping wolves. People have helped gray wolves return to Yellowstone National Park. Wolves have not lived there for 60 years. People have also helped red wolves return to areas in the southeastern United States. Wolves have not lived there for 100 years. This is good news for wolves—they're making a comeback!

Wolf pups

Something to Cheer About

People are helping wolves survive by putting them in new places to live. Sometimes this can cause problems. Wolves may kill animals on farms, such as sheep. When that happens, farmers aren't cheering.

But now people are trying to solve these problems. Farmers can get paid back if wolves kill any of their animals. People are also trying to keep the farm animals safe from wolves by putting up electric fences or having guard dogs. If people continue to try to help wolves and the people who live near them, everybody wins. Now that's something to cheer about!

Wolves Scholastic Professional Books

Name _____   Date _____

The Evening Howl

WOLF PUZZLES

Blaze a Trail Home

Blaze is the name of the pack leader. Blaze needs help leading his pack home. Follow the instructions to show the way home.

Color the squares with the smaller paws black.

Color the squares with the smaller trees brown.

Color the squares with the larger paws green.

Color the squares with the larger trees red.

Do you see the path? It forms a number 2.

Draw a line to show the path.

Word Scramble

Read the words in each row. Circle the word in each row that is not about wolves. Find the letter above the circled word. Write the letters on the lines in order from 1 to 4. The letters will spell the answer to the riddle!

	O	L	W	R	H
1.	red fox	basset hound	coyote	jackal	lion
2.	feathers	teeth	paws	tail	fur
3.	deer	bison	mushrooms	moose	fish
4.	gray	green	brown	white	black

What is a wolf's favorite holiday? __ __ __ __-o-ween

1 2 3 4

Wolf Resources

BOOKS FOR STUDENTS

Amazing Wolves, Dogs, and Foxes, by Mary Ling (Knopf, 1991), is an Eyewitness Juniors book that presents an interesting overview of canids as well as photographs, art, and fun facts.

The Call of the Wolves, by Jim Murphy (Turtleback, 1994), shares the adventure of a young arctic wolf that has been separated from its pack.

Dream Wolf, by Paul Goble (Alladin Picture Books, 1997), is the story of two Plains Indian children who are helped home by a friendly wolf when they are lost.

The Eyes of Gray Wolf, by Jonathan London (Chronicle, 1993), follows Gray Wolf as he encounters a new pack and finds a mate.

Gray Wolf, Red Wolf, by Dorothy Hinshaw Patent (Clarion, 1990), offers a detailed look at North America's two species of wolves.

Once a Wolf: How Wildlife Biologists Brought Back the Gray Wolf, by Stephen R. Swinburne (Houghton Mifflin, 1999), is a Scientists in the Field title that features excellent photographs by Jim Brandenburg.

Peter and the Wolf, by Sergei Prokofiev (Viking, 1982), differs from other versions of the classic story in that it features a more realistic portrayal of the wolf.

Wolves, by Seymour Simon (HarperTrophy, 1995), contains intriguing photographs and helps dispel myths about wolves.

BOOKS FOR TEACHERS

Behavior of Wolves, Dogs, and Related Canids, by Michael W. Fox (Harper and Row, 1971), takes a scientific look at what makes canids tick.

Never Cry Wolf, by Farley Mowat (Bantam, 1984), shares a touching and humorous account of one scientist's adventure studying wolves in the wild.

"Return of the Gray Wolf" is an article by Douglas H. Chadwick that appeared in the May 1998 issue of *National Geographic.*

Wolf: Spirit of the Wild: A Celebration of Wolves in Word and Images, edited by Diana Landau (Sterling Publications, 2000), offers a comprehensive look at wolves in history, science, culture, and art.

Wolves, by R. D. Lawrence (Sierra Club Books, 1990), was written for older children but offers a thorough account of a wolf's life that is sure to be of interest to teachers as well.

CLASSROOM RESOURCES

Discovering Wolves: A Nature Activity Book and ***Timber Wolf Tracks: A K–4 Curriculum Guide*** are available from the Sigurd Olson Environmental Institute, Northland College, Ashland, WI 54806. The group also rents audiovisual programs and has a book for teachers: *Beyond Little Red Riding Hood: A Resource Directory for Teaching About Wolves.* Write to them for more information or visit their Web site at **www.northland.edu/.**

The Wonder of Wolves: A Story and Activities, produced by the Denver Museum of Science and Nature (Roberts Rinehart, 1997), contains an original story and activities complete with ready-to-go reproducibles.

WEB SITES

BoomerWolf is a kids' site with interactive games, adventures, and the character, BoomerWolf, who will answer kids' questions at **www.boomerwolf.com.**

Defenders of Wildlife: Wolf Update at **www.defenders.org** features wolf news as well as information about conservation efforts. Go to the Wildlife at Risk link and select "wolves."

International Wolf Center allows children to track wolf packs online, find out facts about wolves, and view lots of wolf images. Go to **www.wolf.org.**

U.S. Fish and Wildlife Service offers lots of information about endangered species, including wolves. It's at **www.fws.gov.**

"Wild Animal Watch: Wolves" at **http://teacher.scholastic.com/ wolves** is Scholastic's site where kids can read interviews with wolf scientists, find out wolf facts, listen to wolf howls, view wolf artwork, and read scientists' journals about their work with both red and gray wolves.

Wolf Education and Research Center at **www.wolfcenter.org** features general wolf information as well as information about the Sawtooth pack, a group of captive wolves that you can monitor online.

ADOPT A WOLF

The following groups allow you to "adopt" wolves in exchange for donations that support wolf protection.

Defenders of Wildlife, 1101 14th St., NW, Ste. 1400, Washington, DC 20005. **www.defenders.org /adoptfrm./html.**

The Wolf Education and Research Center, 418 Nez Perce, P.O. Box 217, Winchester, ID 83555. **www.wolfcenter.org.**

Timber Wolf Alliance, Sigurd Olson Environmental Institute, Northland College, Ashland, WI 54806. **www.northland.edu/soei/twa.**

Timber Wolf Information Network, E110 Emmons Creek Rd., Waupaca, WI 54981. **www.timberwolfinformation.org.**